teacher's friend publications

November

a creative idea book
for the
elementary teacher

written and illustrated
by
Karen Sevaly

Copyright © 1989
Teacher's Friend Publications, Inc.
All rights reserved
Printed in the United States of America
Published by Teacher's Friend Publications, Inc.
7407 Orangewood Drive, Riverside, CA 92504

ISBN 0-943263-02-6

TO TEACHERS AND CHILDREN EVERYWHERE.

Table of Contents

Making the Most of It!

WHAT IS IN
THIS BOOK:

You will find the following in each monthly idea book from Teacher's Friend Publications:

1. A calendar listing every day of the month with a classroom idea.

2. At least four new student awards to be sent home to parents.

3. Three new bookmarks that can be used in your school library or given to students by you as "Super Student Awards."

4. Numerous bulletin board ideas and patterns pertaining to the particular month.

5. Easy to make craft ideas related to the monthly holidays.

6. Dozens of activities emphasizing not only the obvious holidays but also chapters related to such subjects as: Election Day and Children's Book Week.

7. Crossword puzzles, word finds, creative writing pages, booklet covers and much more.

8. Scores of classroom management techniques, the newest and the best.

HOW TO USE
THIS BOOK:

Every page of this book may be duplicated for individual classroom use.

Some pages are meant to be used as duplicating masters and used as student work sheets. Other pages may be copied onto construction paper or used as they are.

If you have access to a print shop, you will find that many pages work well when printed on index paper. This type of paper takes crayons and felt markers well and is sturdy enough to last and last. The wheel pattern and bookmarks are two items that work particularly well on index paper.

Lastly, some pages are meant to be enlarged with an overhead or opaque projector. When we say enlarge, we mean it! Think BIG! Three, four or even five feet is great! Try using colored butcher paper or poster board so you don't spend all your time coloring.

Making the Most of It!

ADDING THE COLOR:

Putting the color to finished items can be a real bother to teachers in a rush.   Try these ideas:

1.   On small areas, water color markers work great.
     If your area is rather large switch to crayons or even colored chalk or pastels.

     (Don't worry, lamination or a spray fixative will keep the color on the work and off of you. No laminator or fixative? That's okay, a little hair spray will do the trick.)

2.   The quickest method of coloring large items is to simply start with colored paper. (Poster board, butcher paper and large construction paper work well.) Add a few dashes of a contrasting colored marker or crayon and you will have it made.

3.   Try cutting character eyes, teeth, etc. from white typing paper and gluing them in place. These features will really stand out and make your bulletin boards come alive.

     For special effects add real buttons or lace. Metallic paper looks great on stars and belt buckles, too.

LAMINATORS:

If you have access to a roll laminator you already know how fortunate you are. They are priceless when it comes to saving time and money. Try these ideas:

1.   You can laminate more than just classroom posters and construction paper. Try various kinds of fabric, wall paper and gift wrapping. You'll be surprised at the great combinations you come up with.

     Laminated classified ads can be used to cut headings for current event bulletin boards. Colorful gingham fabric makes terrific cut letters or scalloped edging. You might even try burlap! It looks terrific on a fall bulletin board.

     (You can even make professional looking bookmarks with laminated fabric or burlap. They are great gift ideas.)

2.   Felt markers and laminated paper or fabric can work as a team. Just make sure the markers you use are permanent and not water based. Oops, make a mistake! That's okay. Put a little ditto fluid on a tissue, rub across the mark and presto, it's gone! (Dry transfer markers work great on lamination, too.)

Making the Most of It!

LAMINATORS:
(continued)

3. Laminating cut-out characters can be tricky. If you have enlarged an illustration onto poster board, simply laminate first and then cut it out with an art knife. (Just make sure the laminator is plenty hot.)

One problem may arise when you paste an illustration onto poster board and laminate the finished product. If your paste-up does not cover 100% of the illustration, the poster board may separate from it after laminating. To avoid this problem, paste your illustration onto poster board that measures slightly larger. This way, the lamination will help hold down your illustration.

4. Have you ever laminated student-made place mats, crayon shavings, tissue paper collages, or dried flowers? You'll be amazed at the variety of creative things that can be laminated and used in the classroom, or as take-home gifts.

DITTO MASTERS:

Many of the pages in this book can be made into masters for duplicating. Try some of these ideas for best results:

1. When using new masters, turn down the pressure on the duplicating machine. As the copies become light, increase the pressure. This will get longer wear out of both the master and the machine.

2. If the print from the back side of your original comes through the front when making a master or photocopy, slip a sheet of black construction paper behind the sheet. This will mask the unwanted black lines and create a much better copy.

3. Trying to squeeze one more run out of that worn master can be frustrating. Try lightly spraying the inked side of the master with hair spray. For some reason, this helps the master put out those few extra copies.

4. Several potential masters in this book contain instructions for the teacher. Simply cover the type with correction fluid or a small slip of paper before duplicating.

BULLETIN BOARDS:

Creating clever bulletin boards for your classroom need not take fantastic amounts of time and money. With a little preparation and know-how you can have different boards each month with very little effort. Try some of these ideas:

1. Background paper should be put up only once a year. Choose colors that can go with many themes and holidays. A black butcher paper background will look terrific with springtime butterflies or a spooky Halloween display.

2. Butcher paper is not the only thing that can be used to cover the back of your board. You might like to try the classified ad section of the local newspaper for a current events board. Or how about colored burlap? Just fold it up at the end of the year to reuse again.

3. Wallpaper is another great background cover. Discontinued rolls can be purchased for next to nothing at discount hardware stores. Most can be wiped clean and will not fade like construction paper. (Do not glue wallpaper directly to the board, just staple or pin in place.)

ON-GOING BULLETIN BOARDS:

Creating the on-going bulletin board can be easy. Give one of these ideas a try.

1. Choose one board to be a calendar display. Students can change this monthly. They can do the switching of dates, month titles and holiday symbols. Start the year with a great calendar board and with a few minor changes each month it will add a sparkle to the classroom.

2. A classroom tree bulletin board is another one that requires very little attention after September. Cut a large bare tree from brown butcher paper and display it in the center of the board. (Wood-grained adhesive paper makes a great tree, also.) Children can add fall leaves, flowers, apples, Christmas ornaments, birds, valentines, etc., to change the appearance each month.

ON-GOING
BULLETIN BOARDS:
(continued)

3. Birthday bulletin boards, classroom helpers, school announcement displays and reading group charts can all be created once before school starts and changed monthly with very little effort. With all these on-going ideas, you'll discover that all that bulletin board space seems smaller than you thought.

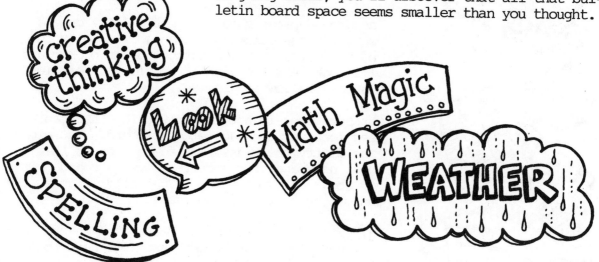

LETTERING AND
HEADINGS:

Not every school has a letter machine that produces perfect 2" or 4" letters from construction paper. (There is such a thing, you know.) The rest of us will just have to use the old stencil and scissor method. But wait, there is an easier way!

1. Don't cut individual letters. They are difficult to pin up straight, anyway. Instead, hand print bulletin board titles and headings onto strips of colored paper. When it is time for the board to come down, simply roll it up to use again next year.

   Use your imagination. Try cloud shapes and cartoon bubbles. They will all look great.

2. Hand lettering is not that difficult, even if your printing is not up to penmanship standards. Print block letters with a felt marker. Draw big dots at the ends of each letter. This will hide any mistakes and add a charming touch to the overall effect.

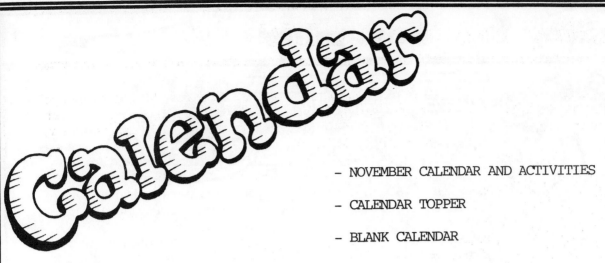

Calendar

- NOVEMBER CALENDAR AND ACTIVITIES

- CALENDAR TOPPER

- BLANK CALENDAR

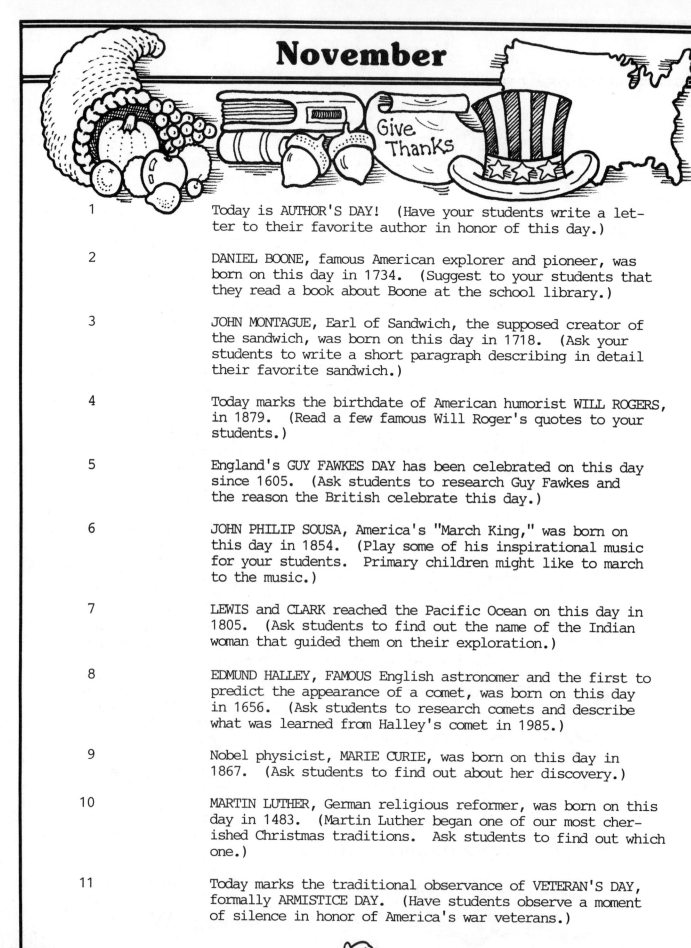

November

1   Today is AUTHOR'S DAY! (Have your students write a letter to their favorite author in honor of this day.)

2   DANIEL BOONE, famous American explorer and pioneer, was born on this day in 1734. (Suggest to your students that they read a book about Boone at the school library.)

3   JOHN MONTAGUE, Earl of Sandwich, the supposed creator of the sandwich, was born on this day in 1718. (Ask your students to write a short paragraph describing in detail their favorite sandwich.)

4   Today marks the birthdate of American humorist WILL ROGERS, in 1879. (Read a few famous Will Roger's quotes to your students.)

5   England's GUY FAWKES DAY has been celebrated on this day since 1605. (Ask students to research Guy Fawkes and the reason the British celebrate this day.)

6   JOHN PHILIP SOUSA, America's "March King," was born on this day in 1854. (Play some of his inspirational music for your students. Primary children might like to march to the music.)

7   LEWIS and CLARK reached the Pacific Ocean on this day in 1805. (Ask students to find out the name of the Indian woman that guided them on their exploration.)

8   EDMUND HALLEY, FAMOUS English astronomer and the first to predict the appearance of a comet, was born on this day in 1656. (Ask students to research comets and describe what was learned from Halley's comet in 1985.)

9   Nobel physicist, MARIE CURIE, was born on this day in 1867. (Ask students to find out about her discovery.)

10   MARTIN LUTHER, German religious reformer, was born on this day in 1483. (Martin Luther began one of our most cherished Christmas traditions. Ask students to find out which one.)

11   Today marks the traditional observance of VETERAN'S DAY, formally ARMISTICE DAY. (Have students observe a moment of silence in honor of America's war veterans.)

November

12   Today marks the birthdate of ELIZABETH CADY STANTON, American leader of the women's sufferage movement, in 1815. (Discuss changes that have taken place in the women's movement in recent years with your students.)

13   Scottish poet and novelist, ROBERT LOUIS STEVENSON, was born on this day in 1850. (Read a poem or two to your students from Stevenson's A Child's Garden of Verses.)

14   ROBERT FULTON, American inventor of the steamboat, was born on this day in 1765. (Ask students to find out how his invention changed American transportation and industry.)

15   SCHICHI-GO-SAN is celebrated today in Japan. Young children visit shrines and offer gifts of thanksgiving. (Ask students to locate Japan on the classroom map.)

16   Today is SADIE HAWKINS DAY. Women first, is the rule of the day. (Let the girls of your class be first today, first on the bus, first on the playground, first to go to lunch, etc.)

17   The SUEZ CANAL, in Egypt, was opened on this day in 1869. (Ask students to find the Suez Canal on the classroom map and discuss the importance of this waterway to world trade.)

18   Today marks the birthdate of MICKEY MOUSE in 1928. (Ask students to find out which cartoon was Mickey's first.)

19   Today is DISCOVERY DAY in Puerto Rico. Christopher Columbus discovered this island in 1493. (Teach your students to say Hello, "Buenos Dias," Goodbye, "Adios" and Thank you, "Gracias" in spanish to celebrate.)

20   PEREGRINE WHITE, the first child born in the colonies of English parents , was born on this day in 1620. (Discuss with your students the hardships that befell the pilgrims that first winter.)

21   Today is WORLD HELLO DAY! (Teach your students to say hello in three or four different languages.)

22   U.S. President JOHN F. KENNEDY was assassinated on this day in 1963. (Display books about Kennedy's life in a silent reading area of your classroom.)

23   The 14th President of the United States, FRANKLIN PIERCE, was born on this day in 1804. (Pierce never wanted to be President. Ask students to find out more about this President.)

24   FATHER JUNIPERO SERRA, founder of the California missions, was born on this day in 1713. (Ask students to trace his route and locate his missions along the California coast using the classroom map.)

25   The American industrialist, ANDREW CARNEGIE, was born on this day in 1835. (Carnegie gave away most of his wealth to worthy charities and causes. Ask students to research his accomplishments.)

26   Today is SOJOURNER TRUTH MEMORIAL DAY. (Honor this early civil rights leader by finding out more about her.)

27   HENRY BACON, American architect, was born on this day in 1866. (Ask students to find out what historical monuments and buildings were designed by Bacon.)

28   The first UNITED STATES POST OFFICE opened its doors on this day in 1783. (Ask students to learn their zip codes in commemoration.)

29   LOUISA MAY ALCOTT, American novelist, was born on this day in 1832. (Suggest her book, <u>Little Women</u> for student reading during Children's Book Week.)

30   SAMUAL CLEMENS, American author, was born on this day in 1835. (Ask students to find out what pen name was used by Clemens.)

ELECTION DAY – The first Tuesday in November.

THANKSGIVING DAY – The fourth Thursday in November.

CHILDREN'S BOOK WEEK – The third week of November.

Calendar Topper

November

sun	mon	tue	wed	thu	fri	sat

Harvest Activities

- HARVEST FESTIVALS

- CREATIVE WRITING PAGE

- PLACE CARDS

- PENCIL TOPPERS

- BOOKMARKS

- AWARDS AND CERTIFICATES

- CORNUCOPIA

- COLOR PAGE

Harvest Festivals

In the United States, Thanksgiving has always been viewed as a uniquely American festival. Our first Thanksgiving was observed by the Pilgrims in the year 1621. The Pilgrims, however, had many ancient Thanksgiving customs to follow. For thousands of years thanksgiving and harvest festivals have been celebrated in many countries throughout the world.

The following descriptions of harvest festivals and their countries of origin can be used as a base for class discussion.

GREECE
"Harvest to the Goddess Demeter" - The Greeks made yearly offerings to the goddess of the soil, Demeter. This feasting time was regarded so highly that it was even held during times of war. Soldiers would cease fighting and joyfully march through the streets carrying stalks of grain. This three-day festival was held in the month of November.

ISRAEL
"Hebrew Feast of the Tabernacles" or "Sukkot" - This Jewish harvest festival falls in the month of September or October. During Sukkot, families build little huts or tents to represent the huts the Jews used when living in the wilderness. Family members decorate the tiny huts with flowers and fruits. This is a great day for feasting and thanking God for the harvest.

CHINA
"Harvest Moon" - This harvest festival is also known as the birthday of the moon. This is a special time of feasting and giving thanks. In celebration, women bake traditional "moon cakes." One year, during a war, village women baked messages into the "moon cakes" that were then delivered to the soldiers. These "moon cake" messages helped them defeat their enemy.

IROQUOIS NATION
"Harvest Ceremony" - The Iroquois tribes celebrated the spirits of many fruits and crops. They particularly observed and gave thanks for the strawberry, raspberry and corn. They observed their thanksgiving with prayers for future great harvests.

ENGLAND
"Harvest Home" - Churches throughout England observe this lovely festival by decorating with flowers, fruits and vegetables. Often, people from entire villages follow the last harvest wagon in from the fields. They walk behind the wagon throughout the town singing songs and hymns.

Creative Writing

Using the letters T-H-A-N-K-S-G-I-V-I-N-G,
list the reasons you are thankful.

T
H
A
N
K
S
G
I
V
I
N
G

NOVEMBER

cut

fold

Happy
Thanksgiving

_____
name

fold

Happy
Thanksgiving

cut

_____
name

Reproduce these "Pencil Toppers" onto construction paper. Color and cut out. Use an art knife to cut through the Xs.

Slide a pencil through both Xs, as shown.

Use as classroom, holiday or birthday treats.

Bookmarks

Don't Forget to VOTE!

HARVEST A WORLD OF LEARNING... **READ!**

Don't be a Turkey...

Read a Book!

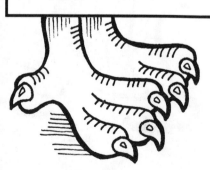

Awards

_____
Name

WAS A PERFECT STUDENT TODAY!

_____
Date

_____
Date

_____
Name

REALLY DID A GREAT JOB TODAY!

_____

_____

_____
Name

HARVESTED A WORLD OF LEARNING TODAY!

_____

_____

_____

_____

_____
Date

_____
Name

WAS A TERRIFIC STUDENT TODAY!

_____

_____

_____

Certificate of Award

presented to

_____

in recognition of

_____

PRINCIPAL

_____

TEACHER

Certificate Of Merit

is awarded this certificate in recognition of

_____

date

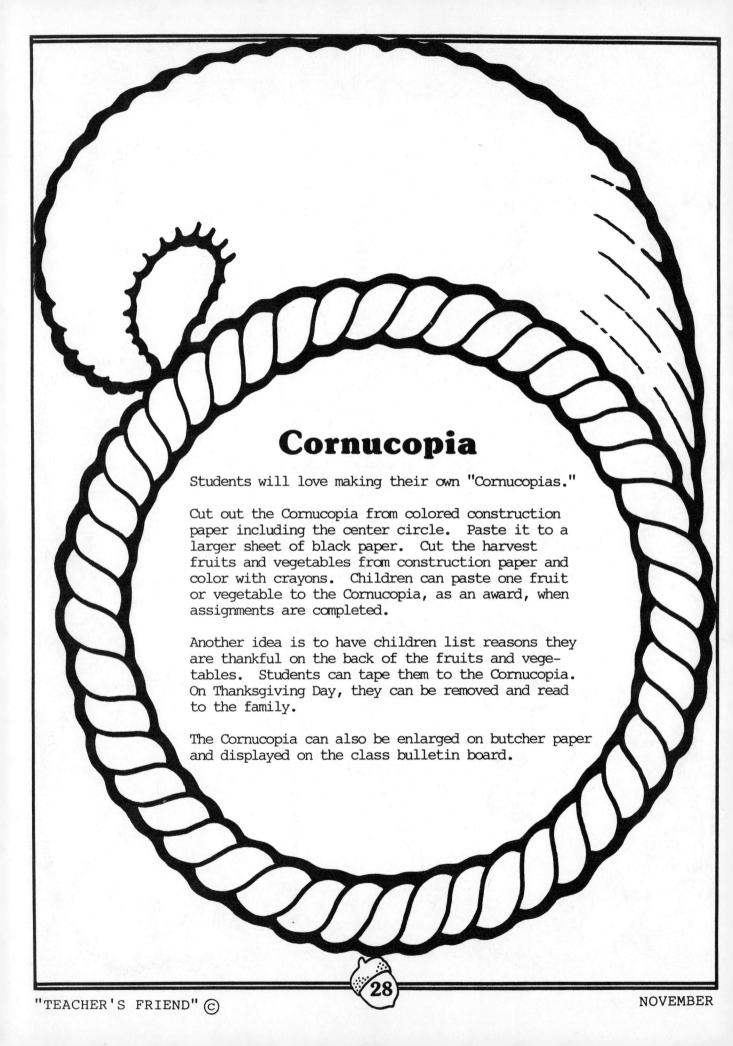

Cornucopia

Students will love making their own "Cornucopias."

Cut out the Cornucopia from colored construction paper including the center circle. Paste it to a larger sheet of black paper. Cut the harvest fruits and vegetables from construction paper and color with crayons. Children can paste one fruit or vegetable to the Cornucopia, as an award, when assignments are completed.

Another idea is to have children list reasons they are thankful on the back of the fruits and vegetables. Students can tape them to the Cornucopia. On Thanksgiving Day, they can be removed and read to the family.

The Cornucopia can also be enlarged on butcher paper and displayed on the class bulletin board.

NOVEMBER

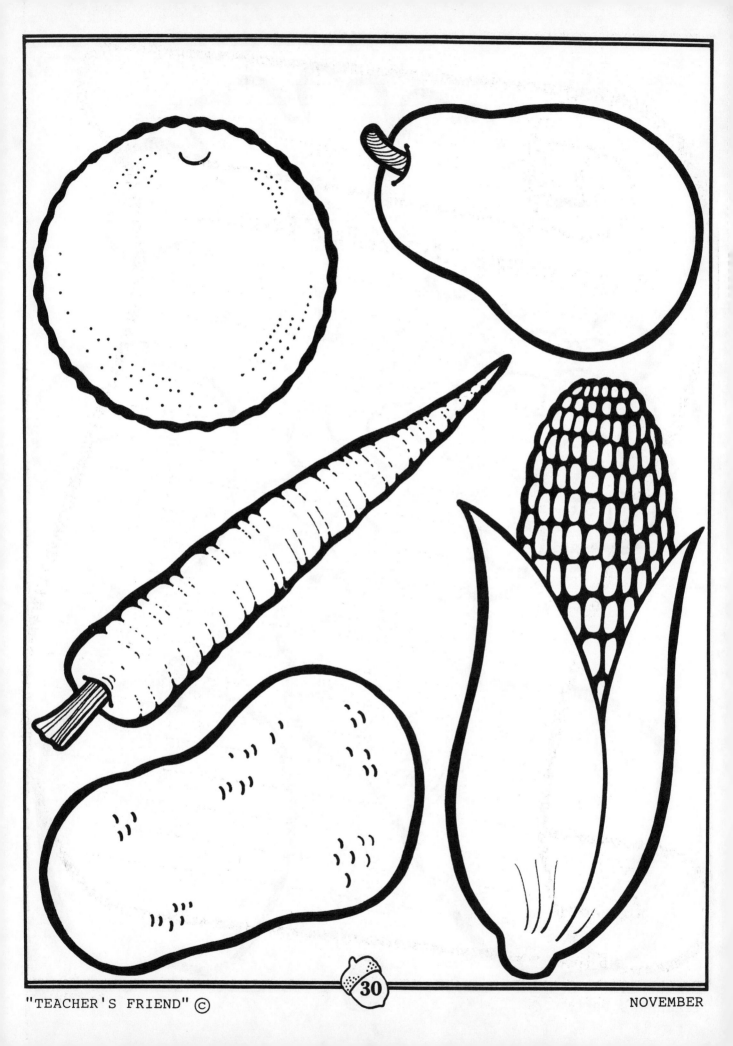

NOVEMBER

Name _____

I am most thankful for.....

Harvest Color Page

TEACHERS: Add your own math problems to this Horn of Plenty. Children can color the picture when work is completed.

Pilgrims and Indians

- PILGRIM STORY
- PILGRIM COSTUMES
- FINGER PUPPETS
- STORY CHARACTERS
- PILGRIM AND INDIAN CHILDREN
- INDIAN CHIEF
- MATCHING PILGRIMS
- CREATIVE WRITING

NOVEMBER

The Pilgrim Story

The Pilgrims, living in England, were unhappy over events taking place in their homeland. There was much religious persecution. King James would not allow them to attend the church of their choice. Because of this, the Pilgrims decided to leave England and find a place that would let them worship God in their own way. The Pilgrims set sail for Amsterdam and finally settled in Leydon, Holland, where they were warmly welcomed.

They soon realized, however, that they could not stay in Holland unless they were willing to give up their English customs and language. The decision was made to set sail for North America where they could establish their own community and keep the English language.

After much difficulty, they were able to finance and supply two small ships, the "Speedwell" and the "Mayflower." They then began their journey across the Atlantic Ocean. Unfortunately, the "Speedwell" soon began developing a leak and both ships had to return to port. On September 6, 1620, the "Mayflower" set sail alone with 102 people aboard.

This was a difficult time for the Pilgrims. Food was scarce and consisted mostly of salted meat and dry biscuits. They were unable to build fires for either cooking or warmth for fear of burning the ship. Many became ill due to these poor conditions. One happy event did take place during the voyage. A baby was born to the Hopkins family and suitably named "Oceanus."

Land was first sighted on November 11, but it was not until November 21, 1620, that they dropped anchor and began building a settlement near present-day Provincetown, Massachusetts. Before leaving the ship, all of the men signed the "Mayflower Compact" which was an agreement to the fact that they were still loyal to the king of England but would set their own laws to provide for their general good and welfare.

Their first winter was quite difficult. There was little food and simple shelters provided little relief from the cold. The Pilgrims quickly made friends with the Indians who taught them to build stronger houses and hunt for food. When spring finally arrived, the Pilgrims went straight to work plowing the land and planting seeds that they had carried from England. An Indian, named Squanto, became a very good friend and helped with the planting.

When harvest time came, there were more than enough fruits and vegetables to store for the next winter. The Pilgrims were so thankful that they decided to invite their Indian friends for a feast of thanksgiving.

On the day of the feast, the Pilgrims covered the tables with good things to eat from their gardens. The Indians brought wild turkeys, game and shellfish. Before the feast began, everyone bowed their heads and said a prayer of thanksgiving to God. This first Thanksgiving was a joyous occasion which lasted three days.

Today, Thanksgiving is a legal holiday celebrated on the fourth Thursday of November. In millions of homes across America, families reunite and remember to thank God for all the good that has been given them.

NOVEMBER

Pilgrim and Indian Task Cards

PILGRIM TASK CARDS

1. Make a booklet about the first Thanksgiving and compare it to our own Thanksgiving today.

2. Write a menu for the first Thanksgiving dinner. List the foods in alphabetical order.

3. Research the Mayflower. How long was the Mayflower? How many people made the journey? How many days did the trip take?

4. Pretend you are one of the pilgrims. Describe how you are feeling about your new country and write about your experiences during that first year.

5. In your own words, retell the pilgrim's Thanksgiving story.

INDIAN TASK CARDS

1. Explain what role the Indians played in helping the pilgrims that first year.

2. Pretend you are an American Indian in the year 1620. You have just seen some strange people coming to shore from a small boat. How do you feel? What do you do?

3. Research the Indians that helped the pilgrims. Describe their own community and families. Also explain what they wore and what foods they ate.

4. Draw a picture of an Indian village from the information you have learned.

5. Make a booklet about the Indians at the first Thanksgiving. Compare them to American Indians today.

(NOTE: Please remember that when teaching about American Indians, it should be done with great respect for the rich heritage they have contributed to the development of this nation.)

THANKSGIVING IN THE CLASSROOM

Arrange to have a Thanksgiving feast with several other classrooms. Sharing the contributions will help develop an understanding of the true meaning of Thanksgiving.

Ask each classroom to select a food to prepare and share with the other classrooms. Here are some suggestions:

Popcorn
Cranberry Sauce
Corn on the Cob
Homemade Bread
Pumpkin Pudding
Corn Bread

NOVEMBER

Pilgrim Hat and Indian Vest

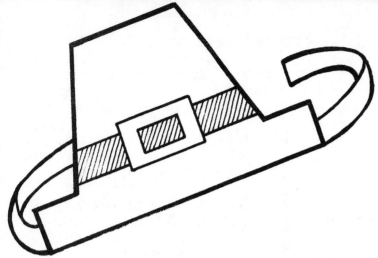

This Pilgrim hat is easily made from 9" X 12" black construction paper. Staple the hat to a paper strip cut to fit a child's head. Add a hat band and a buckle cut from metallic gold adhesive paper.

This simple Indian vest is made from an ordinary grocery bag. Cut a hole for each arm, one for the head and an opening down the front. Children can add their own Indian designs using crayons or paint.

Bags displaying store advertisements can be utilized by carefully turning them inside-out, after you have cut the openings.

Make Indian headbands and feathers from colored construction paper.

Pilgrim Bonnet and Collar

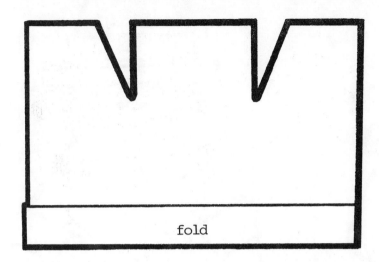

fold

Copy this Pilgrim bonnet onto 12" X 18" white construction paper. Fold over one side, as shown. Bring the back together and staple in place.

Use hair pins to attach to the child's head. Black yarn can also be added to the bonnet and tied under the chin.

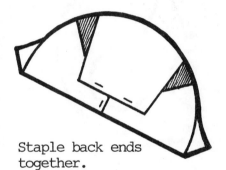

Staple back ends together.

The collar is also cut from 12" X 18" white construction paper. Fold the paper in half and cut a large circle in the center. Join the front of the collar together with a yarn bow.

Cut a notch.

Finger Puppets

NOVEMBER

Pilgrim Children

"TEACHER'S FRIEND" ©   NOVEMBER

NOVEMBER

Indian Children

Indian Children

NOVEMBER

Pilgrim Story Characters

Enlarged, these darling characters can be used in bulletin board displays. You might like to make one of them poster board size and attach it to your classroom door. A word of "Welcome" would be all you would need to greet parents during parent conferences.

The characters can also be used in a flannel board story about Thanksgiving. Cut out and color each illustration. Glue a square of flannel to the back of the picture and apply to the board as you tell the story of the pilgrims.

However you choose to use them, you'll find them to be a real asset to your Thanksgiving activities.

NOVEMBER

Squanto helped the pilgrims
with the planting, fishing
and hunting. He became a
very good friend.

With the help of the Indians, the pilgrims built strong houses.

At harvest time, there were more than enough fruits and vegetables to store for the winter.

The pilgrims gave thanks to God for their many blessings.

During the long voyage, a baby was born to the Hopkins family and appropriately named "Oceanus."

The Mayflower

On September 6, 1620, the "Mayflower" set sail alone with 102 people aboard.

NOVEMBER

Indian Chief

Cut out, color and paste this Indian Chief to colored construction paper. Students can be given paper feathers to add to his headdress as awards for completed work.

Date _____

Work Completed _____

Name _____

Matching Pilgrims

Make several copies of the Pilgrim hats and the two Pilgrim face cards. Add your own problems to the face cards and answers to the appropriate hats. Children match the answer hat to the correct Pilgrim face. Students can do this matching activity at their desk when other work is complete.

Try matching a variety of math problems, homonyms, upper and lower case letters, states and capitals, vowel sounds, word blends, and so on.

NOVEMBER

Creative Writing

NOVEMBER

Turkey Time

- TURKEY FEATHERS
- STAND-UP TURKEY
- CREATIVE TURKEYS
- TURKEY WHEEL
- MOVEABLE TURKEY
- TURKEY PUPPET
- MR. TURKEY

NOVEMBER

Turkey Time

The North American wild turkey was native to our land long before the arrival of the Pilgrims. These wild turkeys were a vital source of food and clothing for many of the east coast Indians. Turkey feathers were also used in the construction of arrows.

These early American turkeys were much different than the domesticated turkeys of today. These wild turkeys were tough, sinewy birds that had to fly to survive. It took many careful hours of cooking to make the meat tender enough to eat.

Some people believe that the turkey was named for the country, "Turkey," but, this isn't so. Actually the name "turkey" came to be as a result of a mistake made by Spanish explorer, Hernando Cortez. During his conquest of Mexico, Cortez discovered a large meaty bird that had been domesticated by the people of Mexico. Cortez took this bird back to Spain, mistaking it for the peacock. The Spaniards began calling this new bird, "toka,' an Indian word for peacock. Later, the word changed to "tukki" and eventually "turkey."

The Spaniards slowly bred the birds to be more meaty and tender. It is said that the turkey was, "one of the most beautiful presents which the New World has made to the Old." Today, more than 500 million turkeys a year find their way to our Thanksgiving tables.

TURKEY TASKS

1. Write the directions for cooking a Thanksgiving turkey. List specific ingredients and cooking times and temperature.

2. Describe what Thanksgiving dinner will be like in the year 2050.

3. Write a thank you note to the member of your family that hosted your Thanksgiving feast.

4. Imagine that you can ask anyone in the world to your Thanksgiving dinner. Who would you invite and why?

5. Write a paragraph on today's turkeys and how they are different from the ones eaten at the first Thanksgiving.

6. To "talk turkey" means to speak bluntly. Write three "talk turkey" sentences about turkeys, themselves.

7. Using ads from the newspaper, plan a Thanksgiving feast for your family. Price each item you would need to buy. Add up your total to find the cost of your Thanksgiving meal.

Turkey Feathers

Enlarge this proud turkey
for a Thanksgiving
bulletin board.

I am thankful for...

Name

Pin the feathers
to the back of
the turkey.

Cut turkey feathers from paper and
have students list things that make
them most thankful.

Stand-up Turkey

Cut out the turkey patterns and color with crayons. Fold the turkey head at the dotted line.

Cut a small flat spot on the bottom of a potato to avoid rolling. Cut a small slit in the potato for the turkey head. Attach the wings and tail with toothpicks.

Set the turkey on the Thanksgiving table for a creative centerpiece.

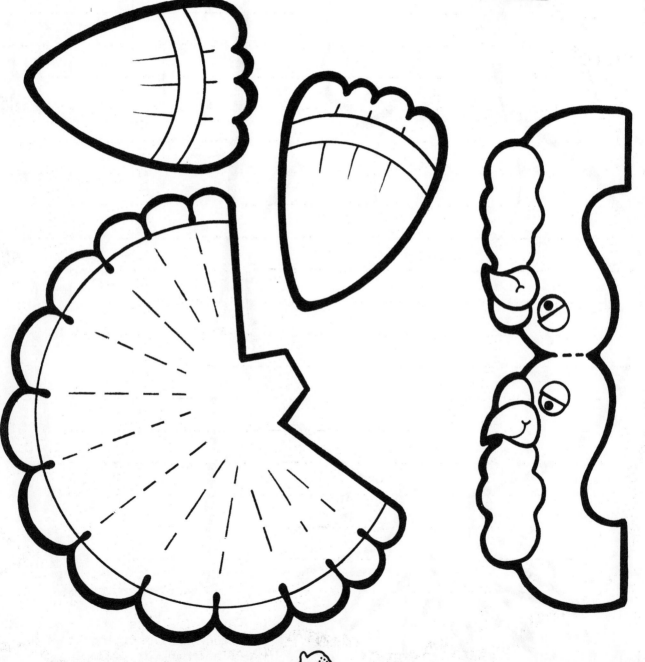

Creative Turkeys

Turkey Wheel

CUT OUT

CUT OUT

Cut out and assemble this "Turkey Wheel" with a brass fastener. Cut out the two rectangles, as shown.

Add your own math problems and answers to the wheel on the next page. Move the turkey wing to reveal the answer.

"TEACHER'S FRIEND" ©   NOVEMBER

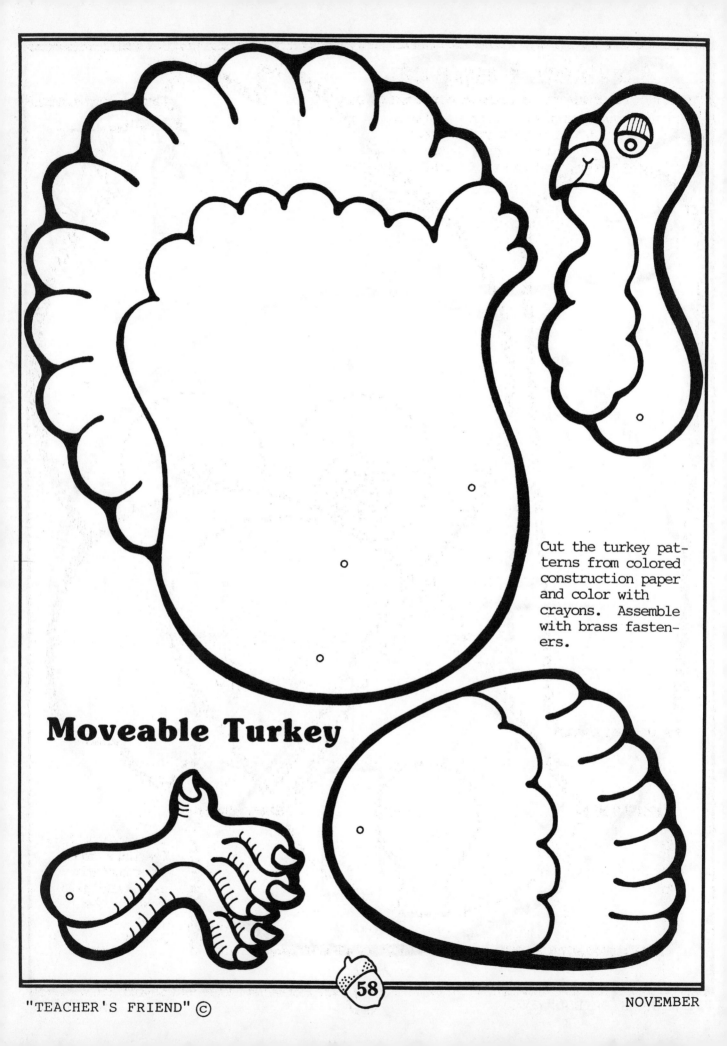

Cut the turkey patterns from colored construction paper and color with crayons. Assemble with brass fasteners.

Moveable Turkey

Turkey Puppet

Cut the turkey patterns from construction paper and glue to a small paper lunch bag. Color with crayons or markers.

Cut several tail feathers from construction paper and glue them to the back of the puppet.

NOVEMBER

Mr. Turkey

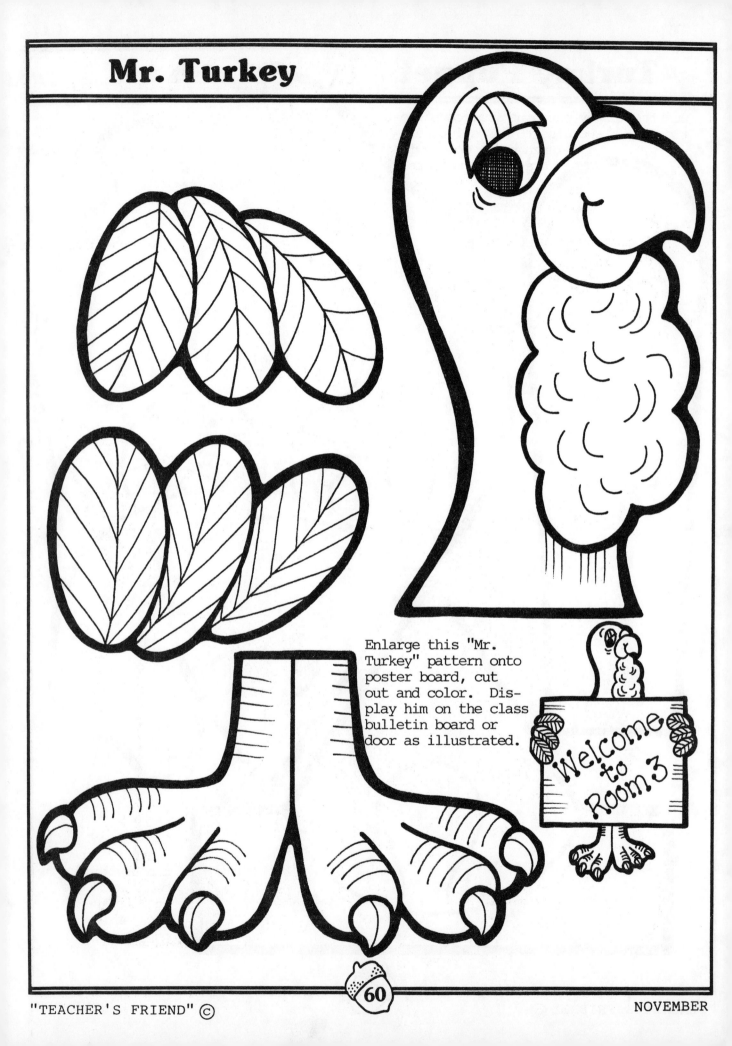

Enlarge this "Mr. Turkey" pattern onto poster board, cut out and color. Display him on the class bulletin board or door as illustrated.

Welcome to Room 3

Children's Book Week

- BOOK WEEK ACTIVITIES

- MY BOOK REPORT

- BOOK REPORT ALTERNATIVES

- BOOK WHEEL

- FOOTPRINTS

- A WORD ABOUT READING

- READING CONTRACT

- MR. BOOK WORM

(THIRD WEEK IN NOVEMBER)

NOVEMBER

Book Week Activities

BOOKMARK CONTEST - Students will have fun designing their own bookmarks and at the same time giving the school library an abundant supply. Give each child a blank bookmark pattern. Instruct them to use only black markers or pens for the artwork. Ask them to think of a catchy jingle or saying that can be printed and then illustrated on the marker. As the bookmarks are submitted, display them in the library. A panel of teachers can judge the contest. Give prize ribbons to the top three winners. The winning bookmark can be duplicated or printed on index paper for use by all students.

NEW BOOK JACKETS - Many books are never checked out because their jackets are worn or unattractive. Instruct students to get a book from the library that they would like to refurbish with a new book jacket. (The book must be read before jackets are made.) Jackets can be made with large sheets of construction paper. Have students draw scenes or characters from the book with crayons or colored markers. Make sure that the title and author's name are clearly labeled on both the front and spine. Laminate the book jackets, if possible. The children will love seeing their book jackets displayed along with the books in the school library.

BOOK SALE - After your students have read a chosen library book have them sell the book to the rest of the class. They may choose to do this in a number of ways, such as; posters, skits and other promotional gimmicks. Student commercials can be especially fun. Make sure the following information is included. Title of the book, author's name, illustrator's name, where the book can be found, and why they should "buy" the book.

MR. BOOK WORM - Color and cut out Mr. Book Worm from the next page. Arrange with the school librarian for your students to conduct a library search.

Hide Mr. Book Worm in a book on the library shelves. Give your students as many clues as necessary to find his location. For example: "Mr. Book Worm has found a giant home in a peachy-keen place. The author is a real Dahl! Can you find me?" (Roald Dahl's James and the Giant Peach is the correct hiding place.

READING KEYS - Cut enough paper keys for every child in class. Write the titles of various books, that your students might enjoy, on each key. Have each student draw a key from a bowl and proceed to find the book in the school library. After the student has read his or her book, the keys can be displayed on the class bulletin board. (The keys also make great bookmarks!)

Students are sure to develop a love for books during Children's Book Week with these reading activities.

Reading Keys and Mr. Book Worm

BOOK TITLE _____

AUTHOR _____

TYPE OF
BOOK _____

Your Name

Mr. Book Worm

My Book Report

Book Title _____

Author _____

_____

_____

_____

_____

_____

_____

_____

_____

_____

_____

_____

☐ **I liked this book.**
☐ **I didn't like this book.**

Why?_____

_____

_____

_____

_____

Book Report Alternatives

1. Choose two characters from the story and write about a conversation they might have.

2. Write a letter to a close friend recommending the book you have just read.

3. Make a list of new, unusual or interesting words or phrases found in your book.

4. Prepare a television commercial about your book. Act out the commercial for your classmates.

5. Draw a cartoon strip using characters from the book.

6. Write a different ending to the story in your book. Do you like your ending better than the author's?

7. Write ten questions which could be used to test other students' understanding of the story. Make sure you include a list of the answers.

8. Explain why you think this book will or will not be read a hundred years from now. Support your opinion by stating specific events in the story.

9. Discuss one particular episode in the story that you remember most. Describe why you think it remains so clear to you.

10. Write a letter to the author of your book. Address it to the publisher's address and mail it.

11. Write a ballad or song about the characters and events in your story. Set the words to the music of a popular song and sing it to the class.

12. Give a dramatic reading of a scene in the book to your classmates.

13. Describe in detail three characters from the story. List reasons why these characters would be nice to know or have as a best friend.

14. Design a poster or book jacket of your book and ask to display it in the school library.

15. Using the title of the book, write a phrase about the book for each letter.

16. Draw a mural depicting the major scenes from the book.

17. After reading an information book, make a scrapbook about the subject.

18. Write a movie script for one of the scenes in your book. You might like to act it out in front of the class with the help of other students.

NOVEMBER

Book Wheel

cut out

Title

NOVEMBER

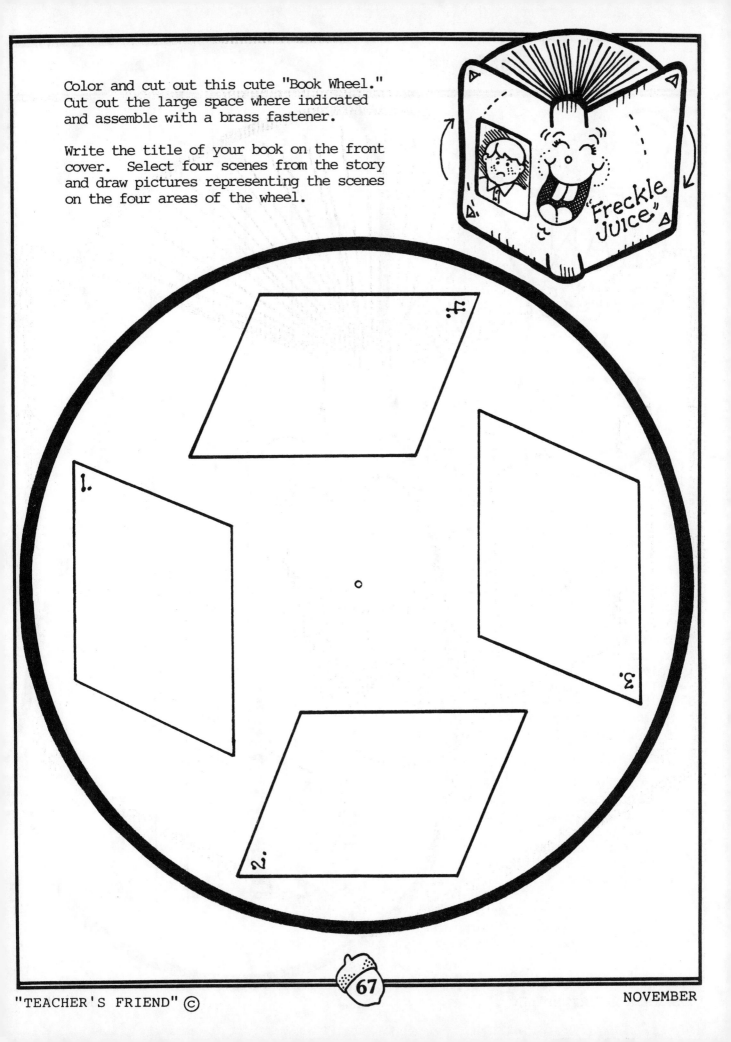

Color and cut out this cute "Book Wheel."
Cut out the large space where indicated
and assemble with a brass fastener.

Write the title of your book on the front
cover. Select four scenes from the story
and draw pictures representing the scenes
on the four areas of the wheel.

"Freckle Juice"

1.

2.

3.

4.

Footprints

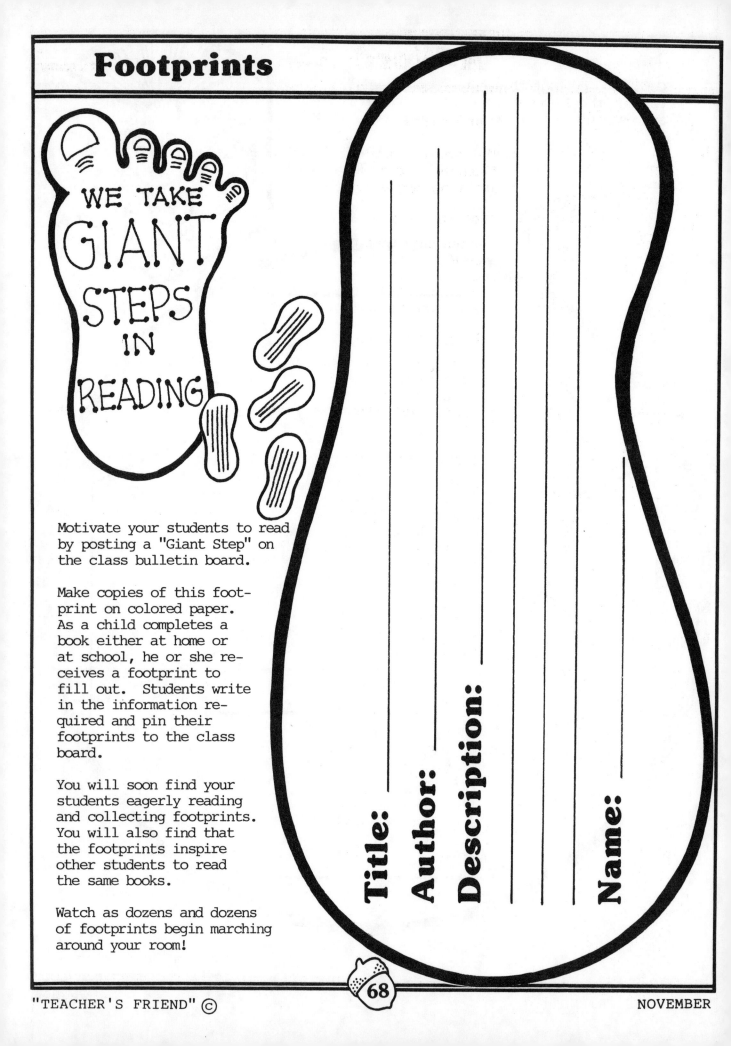

WE TAKE GIANT STEPS IN READING

Motivate your students to read by posting a "Giant Step" on the class bulletin board.

Make copies of this footprint on colored paper. As a child completes a book either at home or at school, he or she receives a footprint to fill out. Students write in the information required and pin their footprints to the class board.

You will soon find your students eagerly reading and collecting footprints. You will also find that the footprints inspire other students to read the same books.

Watch as dozens and dozens of footprints begin marching around your room!

Title:

Author:

Description:

Name:

A Word About Reading

Dear Parents,

The reading patterns you establish at home directly influences your child's ability to do well in school. Here are a few suggestions:

TIME OUT FOR YOUR CHILD

Studies show that parents spend as little as fifteen minutes a day talking, listening and reading to their children. Yet, it is exactly these activities that encourage a child to read. Make sure that you take time out each day to communicate with your child.

READ TO YOUR CHILD

The very best way to help your child become a good reader is to read to and with them at home. The more children read, or are read to, the better. Books are not the only thing to read. Encourage your child to read cereal boxes, street signs, catalogs and magazines.

READING AND WRITING

Teaching a child to write, helps them to read. Keep pencils, paper, chalk and crayons on hand. Young children can learn to form letters and then words. This gives them the opportunity to practice the relationship of letters and sounds. Very young children can dictate to you or an older child. It's also fun to have children write letters to friends and family.

QUIET TIME

The work done in school is reinforced with homework. This gives children time for study and practice. It is very important to set a time for homework and to provide a quiet place where they can do their work. Remember to keep on top of your child's work and stay in touch with your child's teacher.

LIMIT TELEVISION

Most children spend hours in front of the television and only minutes a day reading. Set a limit on television watching and replace it with quality reading time. When television is permitted, follow it with family discussions.

Learning doesn't start or end at school. The more we can work together with reading, the more successful your child will be.

Sincerely,

69

Reading Contract

I promise to read _____ pages

each day until _____ .

I will record my progress on my

Reading Record .

_____
Student

_____
Parent

_____
Teacher

_____
Date

Reading Record

Date	Book Title	Author	Pages Read	Parent's Initials

New Words and Meanings

_____   _____

_____   _____

_____   _____

_____   _____

NOVEMBER

Mr. Book Worm

Color in one section of Mr. Book Worm each time you read the assigned number of pages from your library book.

NOVEMBER

States 'n Capitals

- STATES AND CAPITALS ACTIVITIES

- STATES AND CAPITALS BINGO

- MY STATE BOOK

- IDENTIFY THE STATES

- UNITED STATES MAP

States and Capitals Activities

Fifty individual states make up the great United States of America. Each state is unique in it's own way. Help your students to learn the geographical location of the states and capitals and appreciate their many differences. Try some of these activities with your students.

STATE NAMES - Have students research the origin of each state name. Some state names can be traced to Indian cultures, such as, North and South Dakota. Other states were named for people, such as, Pennsylvania for Willian Penn, the area's first leader. Ask children to write brief paragraphs that can be posted by the state's name on the class bulletin board.

STATE NICKNAMES - Each state has an official or unoffical nickname. Florida is "The Sunshine State" and California is "The Golden State." Assign a state to each student and have them find out their state's nickname. Ask them to find out why this name was chosen and whether or not it seems appropriate. Ask them to come up with some other nicknames that might be more suitable.

COLOR THE U.S. - Give each child a blank map of the United States. Direct them to find various states by listening to your clues, such as, "Alabama touches the Gulf of Mexico. Color it green." Or, "The State of Oregon is on the Pacific Coast. Color it blue." This is a fun way to learn the location and names of all fifty states.

STATE CAPITAL BEE - Using the same rules as a Spelling Bee, divide your class into teams. Verbally give each participant the name of a state. They must correctly identify the capital or leave the game and be seated. Proceed until one team is the winner. Change the game by simply giving capitals and the students answering with the names of the states. This is a clever way to motivate students to learn their states and capitals.

STATES AND CAPITALS BINGO - This is an exciting way to practice memorizing the states and capitals. Give each child a copy of the states or capitals or write them on the chalkboard. Ask students to write any 24 names on his or her bingo card. Use the same directions you might use for regular bingo.

STATE FOLDERS - As a cover for state reports, have students fold a large sheet of construction paper in half and draw an outline of their state on one side. Insert lined paper inside and staple along the folded edge. Cut the booklets along the remaining three sides. Children can then write their state reports inside the folder.

STATES AND CAPITALS BINGO

		FREE		

75

My State Book

Name of State

My Name

I like my State because: _____

My State Book was completed on this date.

"One out of many"

My State's Nickname is:
_____

My State was admitted to the Union in the year:
_____

There are about _____ people that live in my State.

My State's flower is:

My State's bird is:
_____

My State's motto is:
_____
_____

My State is:
_____

This is a drawing of my state.

My State's capital is:
_____

I have shown it's location on the map.

My State is located:

☐ In the West   ☐ In the Northeast

☐ In the Midwest   ☐ In the Southwest

☐ In the South   ☐ Or somewhere else.

Here is my State on the map of the United States.

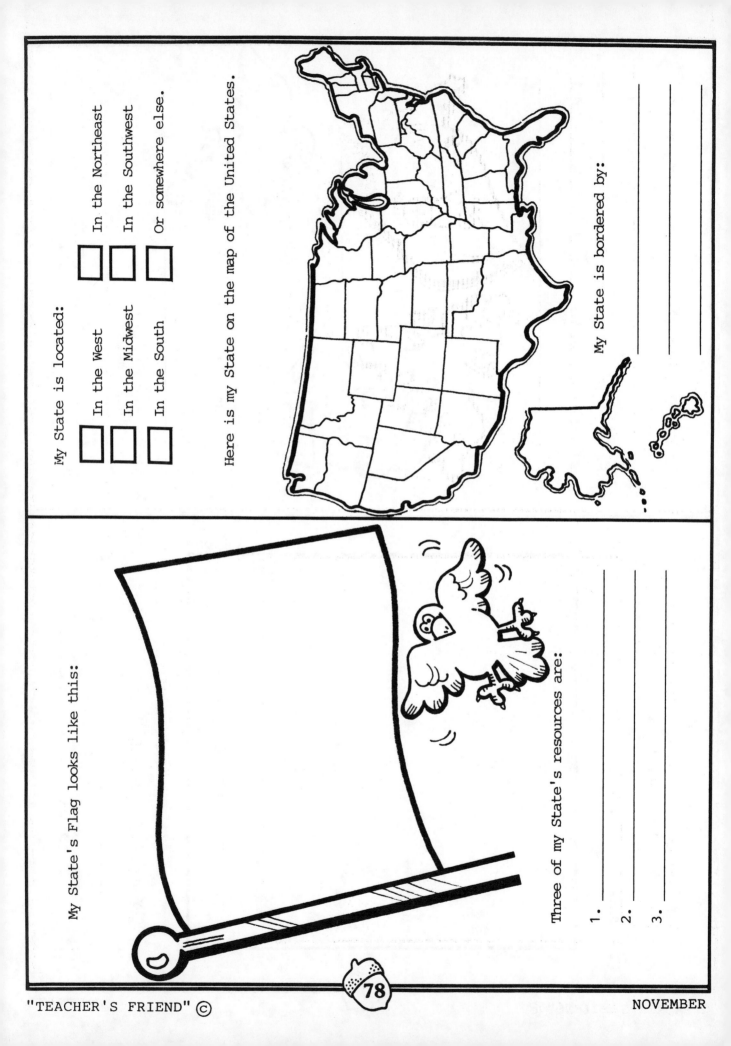

My State is bordered by:

_____

_____

_____

My State's Flag looks like this:

Three of my State's resources are:

1. _____

2. _____

3. _____

My State's main rivers, lakes and mountains are: _____

Historically, my State is famous for: _____

If you ever visit my State make sure you see: _____

My State is famous for many things. Here is a picture of my favorite.

A famous person from my State is: _____

He or she was famous for: _____

NOVEMBER

Identify the States

ALABAMA
ALASKA
ARIZONA
ARKANSAS
CALIFORNIA
COLORADO
CONNECTICUT
DELAWARE
FLORIDA
GEORGIA
HAWAII
IDAHO

ILLINOIS
INDIANA
IOWA
KANSAS
KENTUCKY
LOUISIANA
MAINE
MARYLAND
MASSACHUSETTS
MICHIGAN
MINNESOTA
MISSISSIPPI

MISSOURI
MONTANA
NEBRASKA
NEVADA
NEW HAMPSHIRE
NEW JERSEY
NEW MEXICO
NEW YORK
NORTH CAROLINA
NORTH DAKOTA
OHIO
OKLAHOMA
OREGON

PENNSYLVANIA
RHODE ISLAND
SOUTH CAROLINA
SOUTH DAKOTA
TENNESSEE
TEXAS
UTAH
VERMONT
VIRGINIA
WASHINGTON
WEST VIRGINIA
WISCONSIN
WYOMING

1. _____

2. _____

3. _____

4. _____

5. _____

6. _____

7. _____

8. _____

9. _____

10. _____

11. _____

12. _____

13. _____

14. _____

15. _____

16. _____

17. _____

18. _____

19. _____

20. _____

21. _____

22. _____

23. _____

24. _____

25. _____

26. _____

27. _____

28. _____

29. _____

30. _____

31. _____

32. _____

33. _____

34. _____

35. _____

36. _____

37. _____

38. _____

39. _____

40. _____

41. _____

42. _____

43. _____

44. _____

45. _____

46. _____

47. _____

48. _____

49. _____

50. _____

ACTIVITY 1

80

Identify each state by listing them 1 through 50.

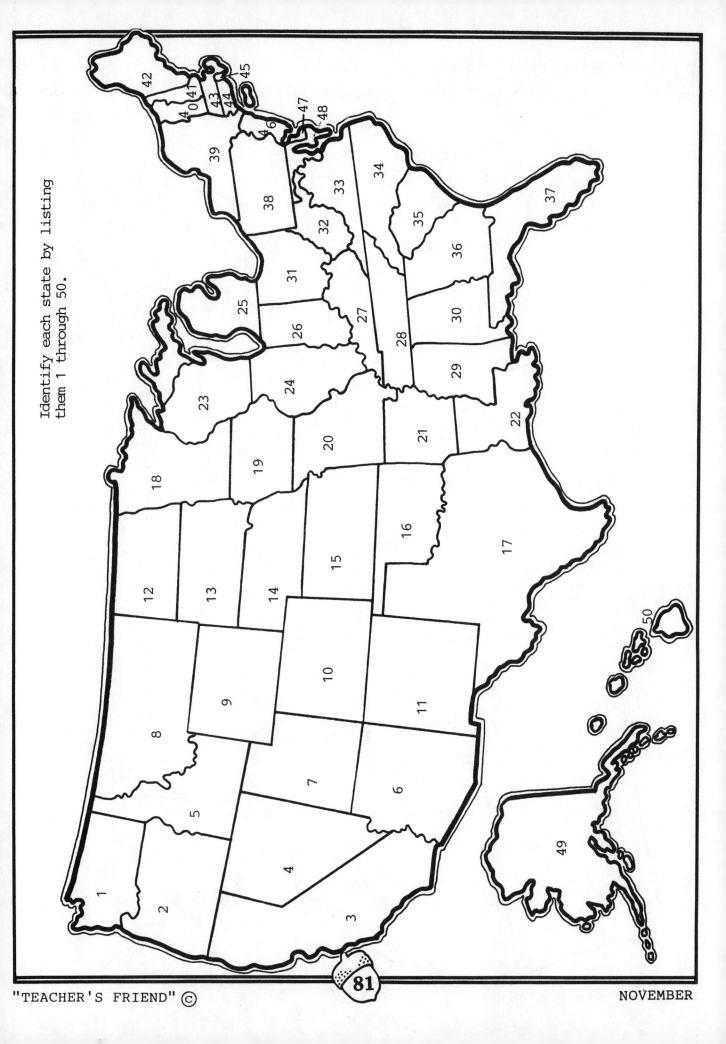

NOVEMBER

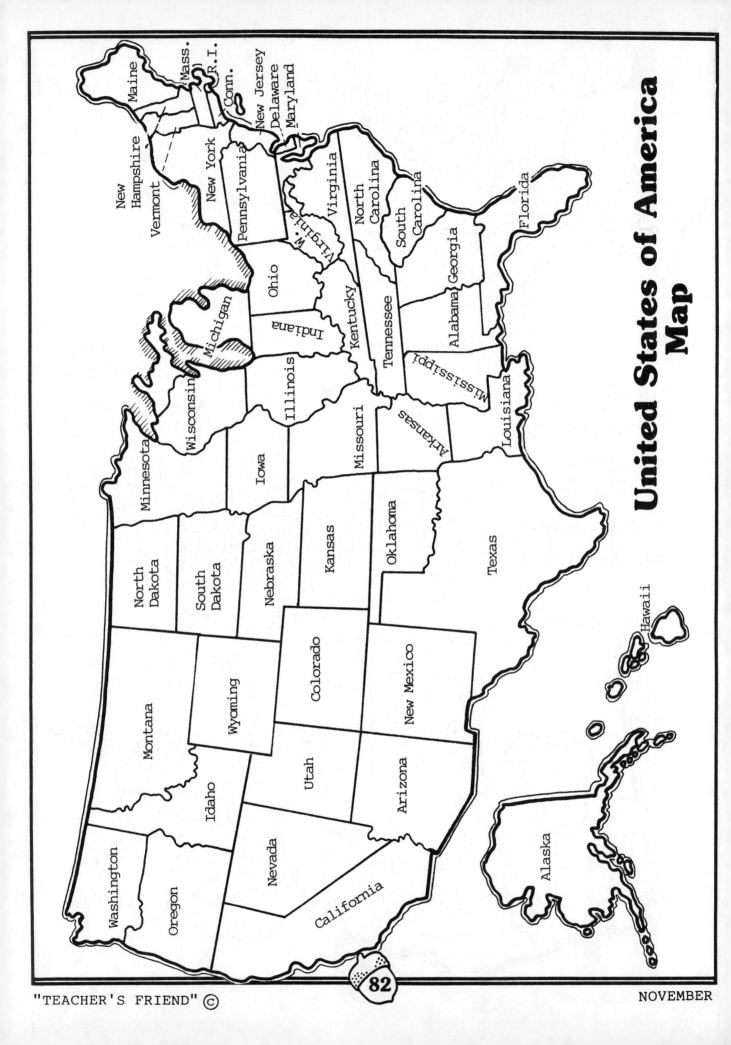

United States of America Map

Election Day

- ELECTION DAY ACTIVITIES

- ELECTION WORD FIND

- EAGLE PATTERN

- UNCLE SAM HAT

- ELECTION GAMEBOARD

- OUR PLEDGE OF ALLEGIANCE

- CAMPAIGN BUTTON

- PRESIDENT CARDS

VOTE
☒ President
☒ Vice-President
USA

Election Day Activities

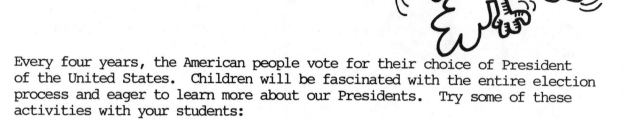

Every four years, the American people vote for their choice of President of the United States. Children will be fascinated with the entire election process and eager to learn more about our Presidents. Try some of these activities with your students:

CLASS DISCUSSIONS - Ask students to list various national and international issues that they think are most important, today. Ask them what they know of the candidate's views on these issues. Ask students their opinions about campaign advertisements and how money is raised to pay for them. Have students collect campaign literature that their parents might receive in the mail. Display the brochures and flyers along with a sample ballot on the class bulletin board.

POLITICAL CARTOONS - Ask students to collect cartoons from local newspapers and analyze their message about the election and today's issues. Students might also like to research political cartoons from the past.

POLLING PLACES - Ask students to find out where the closest polling place to their homes is located. Polls are often located in schools. If your school contains a polling place, arrange for a visit. A poll worker may like to explain the voting process to your students.

Ask students to remind their parents to vote. And don't forget to conduct a secret ballot election in your classroom.

ELECTION NIGHT - Instruct students to watch television coverage of the election results. As students watch the returns with their families, have them write the total votes from each state as it is reported. They might like to use a copy of a U.S. map to record their findings.

ELECTORAL COLLEGE - Help students understand that the President is really elected by the electoral college. In the democratic process, registered voters actually vote for electors who vote for the President. The new President needs 270 electoral votes to win. Ask the students how many votes the winning candidate received in this election. The electors will meet in mid-December to finalize their vote.

ELECTION ANALYSIS - Reveal the outcome of the classroom election and discuss how it agreed or differed from the national election. Ask students to discuss their feelings about the election. What will they most remember? Be sure to continue with current events and discussions about the new President until Inauguration Day in January.

Election Word Find

FIND THESE ELECTION WORDS: NOVEMBER, PRESIDENT, VICE-PRESIDENT, VOTE, BALLOT, DEMOCRAT, REPUBLICAN, CANDIDATE, SPEECH, CAMPAIGN, CONVENTION, INAUGURATION, ELECTION, TERM, NATION.

```
S V R T G H Y K L H N S P E E C H F B N K L Y
X Z A S W Q R T H Y B H R D C V T Y H U J M H
D C X V C A N D I D A T E F H J I I L K M N G
V F G H O S X V B H L J S F T Y N A T I O N P
W R T Y N G H Y U I L N I B G H A R Y U I O P
C V G Y V H U I K J O R D S W E U C V C W Q E
Q S X D E G B F D R T U E D S W G F R A F V B
M L K O N O V E M B E R N O K J U J K M F G T
E L E C T I O N D R T Y T H N J R H G P C V B
R T Y U I S R T G H U J K I O L A G H A C X Z
L P O I O G F D E M O C R A T F T A W I D R T
S G H U N G H Y U I K M N H U Y I F T G E W Y
V I C E P R E S I D E N T F G T O F N N C E T
O F R H G B N M K I L O H B G Y N R F D E W S
T E R M C D F R E P U B L I C A N F R H Y U K
E S C V T G B N J U I K M K L O P M N J H Y T
X D R T G V B H U J M N H Y T R E W Q A S D E
F R G B N J I U H J K L O P M N B V G F R Q W
```

ACTIVITY 2

PAPER BAG EAGLES

This majestic eagle is easily made with a small paper lunch bag. Fill the bag with crumpled paper and close with a rubber band. Color and cut out the eagle head and two wing patterns and glue to the bag.

Pin the eagles to the class bulletin board for a "high flying" display.

85

Eagle Pattern

"TEACHER'S FRIEND" ©   NOVEMBER

Uncle Sam Hat Pattern

Cut this "Uncle Sam" hat from white construction paper. Have children color with crayons. Staple the hat to a strip of paper the correct size to fit a child's head.

Children can wear their hats on election day.

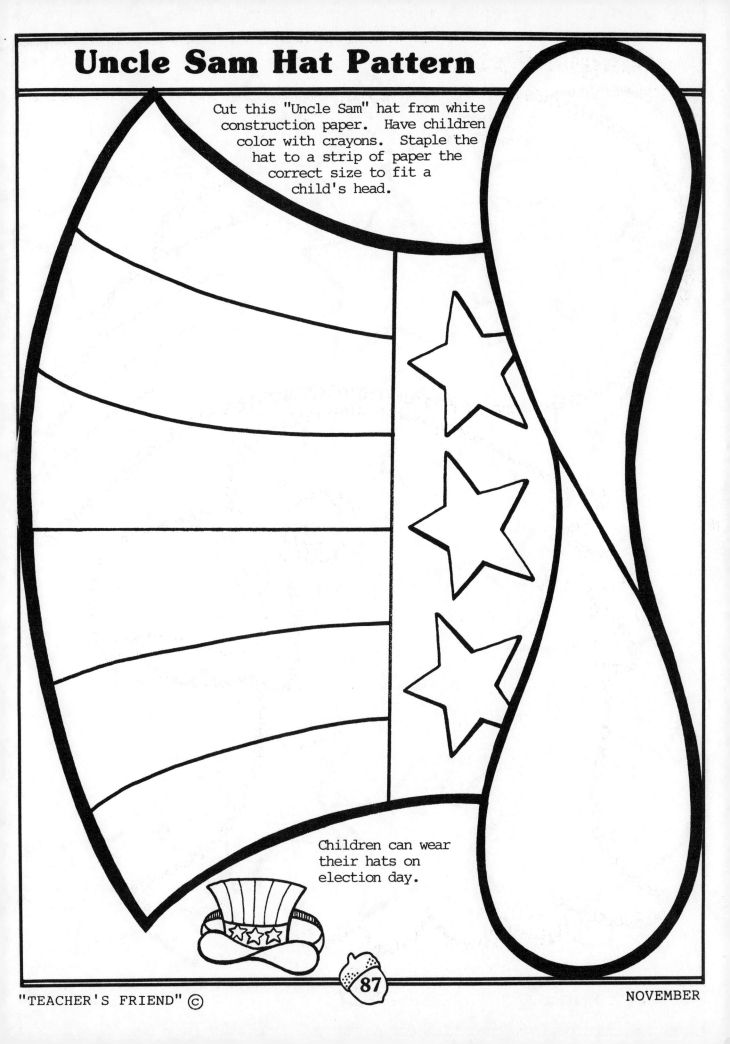

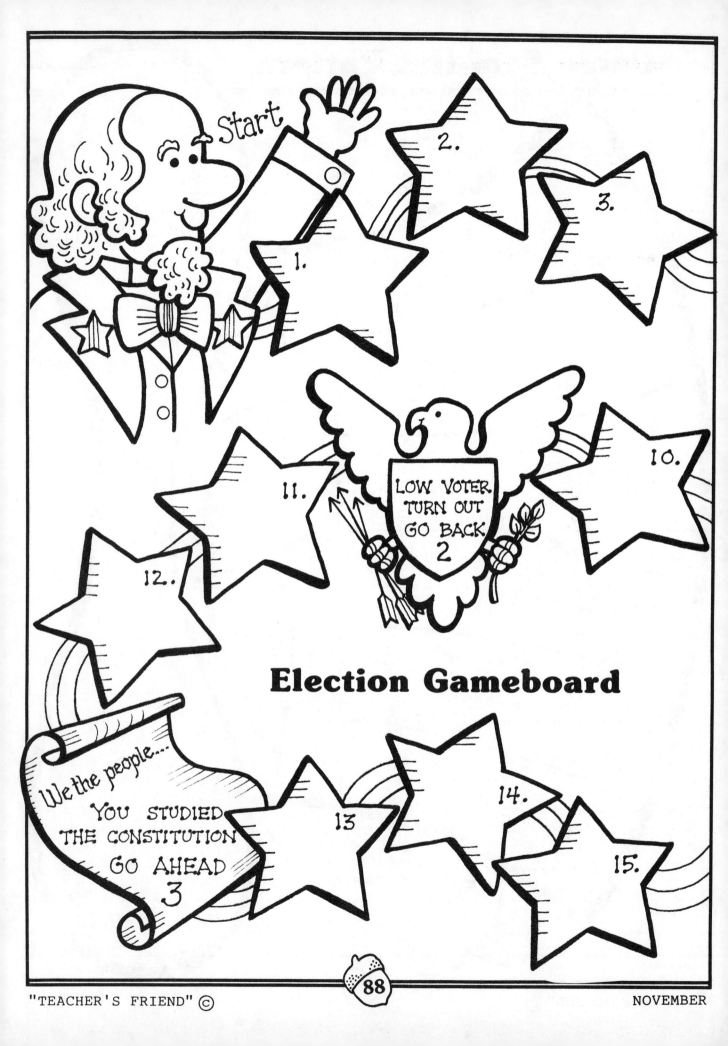

Start

Election Gameboard

NOVEMBER

FORGOT TO VOTE!

GO BACK 3

4.

5.

6.

7.

8.

TEACHERS: Two, three or four children can play this game. Make your own task cards or write math problems, that must be solved, on each star.

9.

YOU HELPED REGISTER VOTERS! MOVE AHEAD 2

Help Uncle Sam Find His Hat!

Assemble both pages on poster board for a fun Election Time gameboard.

16.

17.

18.

Finish!

Our Pledge of Allegiance

I PLEDGE	I PROMISE
ALLEGIANCE	TO BE LOYAL
	(It means we will respect our flag and be loyal or true to our country.)
TO THE FLAG	TO OUR COUNTRY'S SYMBOL
	(The flag always reminds us of our country.)
OF THE UNITED STATES OF AMERICA	OF OUR COUNTRY
	(The United States of America is the name of our country.)
AND TO THE REPUBLIC FOR WHICH IT STANDS	AND TO THE GOVERNMENT OF OUR COUNTRY
	(A republic is a government in which the people elect their leaders.)
ONE NATION UNDER GOD	OUR ONE COUNTRY WHICH BELIEVES IN GOD
	(The term "nation" is another word for "country.")
INDIVISIBLE	CANNOT BE DIVIDED
	(Our country is one which cannot be separated or divided.)
WITH LIBERTY	WITH FREEDOM
	(In America, we believe that all people should have the same rights. We have many freedoms including freedom of speech, religion and peaceable assembly.)
AND JUSTICE FOR ALL.	AND FAIRNESS TO EVERYONE.
	(Each person is to follow the laws of our country. If someone breaks the law, they will be given time to show that he or she did no wrong.)

NOVEMBER

Campaign Button

IF I WERE PRESIDENT.....

NOVEMBER

President Cards

The President Cards can be used in a variety of ways in the classroom. Here are a few suggestions.

RESEARCH CARDS

Make a copy of each card, cut apart and place in a large bowl. Each student draws a card and researches his or her President. Display the research papers along with the picture cards.

ORDINAL NUMBERS ACTIVITY

Cover the ordinal number on each President Card. Have students arrange the cards in the order that each President served office.

PRESIDENT CONCENTRATION

Make two copies of each President Card. Have students lay all of the cards face down. Players take turns turning over two cards at a time, matching the Presidents. The player with the most pairs, wins the game.

BULLETIN BOARD DISPLAY

Display a map of the United States in the center of the class bulletin board. Arrange a copy of the President Cards around the map. Use colored yarn to match each President to his home state.

1st

George Washington
1789-1797

2nd

John Adams
1797-1801

3rd

Thomas Jefferson
1801-1809

4th

James Madison
1809-1817

5th

James Monroe
1817-1825

6th

John Quincy Adams
1825-1829

NOVEMBER

7th

Andrew Jackson
1829-1837

8th

Martin Van Buren
1837-1841

9th

William H. Harrison
1841

10th

John Tyler
1841-1845

11th

James K. Polk
1845-1849

12th

Zachary Taylor
1849-1850

13th

Millard Fillmore
1850-1853

14th

Franklin Pierce
1853-1857

15th

James Buchanan
1857-1861

16th

Abraham Lincoln
1861-1865

17th

Andrew Johnson
1865-1869

18th

Ulysses S. Grant
1869-1877

NOVEMBER

19th

Rutherford B. Hayes
1877-1881

20th

James A. Garfield
1881

21st

Chester A. Arthur
1881-1885

22nd

Grover Cleveland
1885-1889

23rd

Benjamin Harrison
1889-1893

24th

Grover Cleveland
1893-1897

NOVEMBER

25th

William McKinley
1897-1901

26th

Theodore Roosevelt
1901-1909

27th

William H. Taft
1909-1913

28th

Woodrow Wilson
1913-1921

29th

Warren G. Harding
1921-1923

30th

Calvin Coolidge
1923-1929

31st
Herbert Hoover
1929-1933

32nd
Franklin D. Roosevelt
1933-1945

33rd
Harry S. Truman
1945-1953

34th
Dwight D. Eisenhower
1953-1961

35th
John F. Kennedy
1961-1963

36th
Lyndon B. Johnson
1963-1969

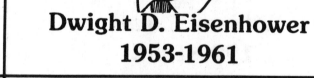

NOVEMBER

37th

Richard M. Nixon
1969-1974

38th

Gerald R. Ford
1974-1977

39th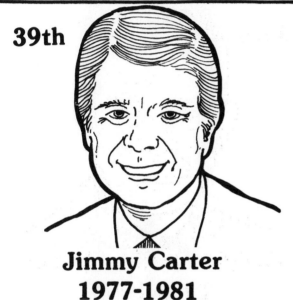

Jimmy Carter
1977-1981

40th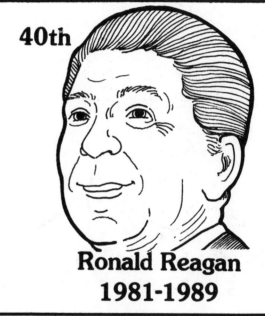

Ronald Reagan
1981-1989

41st

George Bush
1989-

RESEARCH QUESTIONS

1. Where was your President born and what is his birthdate?
2. How old was your President when he was elected to office?
3. How many years did he serve in office? How many terms?
4. Was your President a Democrat or a Republican? Or neither?
5. Did your President have a nickname? What was it?
6. What was his major contribution while in office?
7. Was he married? Did he have children? How many?
8. Name one major national event that happened during your President's term.

Harvest of Learning
Room 12

Sally Ed Mike Maria Lynn Robbie Tom Jimmy Dale Jose Sue Kacie Darren Larry

"TEACHER'S FRIEND" ©

NOVEMBER

Bulletin Boards

ELECTION TIME

Use red, white and blue strip-
ed gift-wrap paper for this
patriotic bulletin board. Students can display Presidential
reports or campaign buttons.

(If you already have a board
covered with either blue or
red butcher paper, simply pin
strips of white paper over the
existing covering.)

PILGRIM AND INDIAN FACES

Let your students draw self portraits on
the back of white paper plates. Headbands,
feathers, pilgrim hats and bonnets can be
cut from colored construction paper. Make
sure each child adds their own name to the
finished product. This is a clever way to
involve your students in welcoming the
Thanksgiving holiday.

PILGRIM FACTS

Display a large paper-cut
"Mayflower" on the class
bulletin board.

Ask students to research
facts about the pilgrims.
Have them write their findings on strips of paper and
display on the board.

(If you have planned ahead
you can use the same ship
for an "Explorers" display.
Simply remove the name
"Mayflower.")

and more....

THE STUFFIN'S IN THE LIBRARY

Display a large paper turkey on the class bulletin board for a clever library display.

Children can display book reports or student-made book jackets.

HANDS-DOWN TURKEY

This delightful turkey will be the center of attention in your classroom. Enlarge the turkey head and feet on posterboard and cut out. Ask students to trace both their hands and feet on red, yellow and orange construction paper. The cut out prints can be pinned to the board to form the body and tail, as illustrated.

Depending on the number of prints, you can make him as large or small as you want.

FEAST OF WORDS

What a great way to introduce November vocabulary words!

Students will love finding "tasty" words to display on this "delicious" bulletin board.

A long scroll of white butcher paper can be used to title the "Feast of Words."

and more!

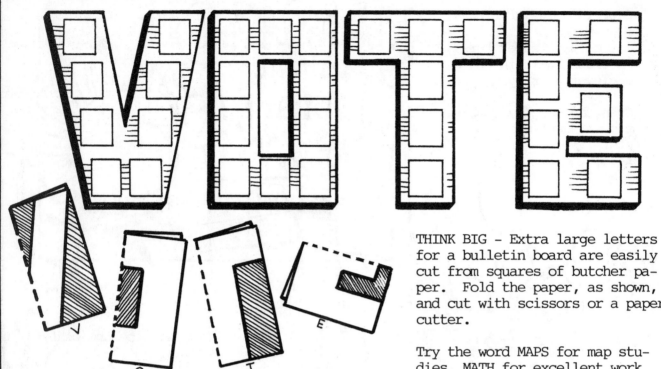

THINK BIG - Extra large letters for a bulletin board are easily cut from squares of butcher paper. Fold the paper, as shown, and cut with scissors or a paper cutter.

Try the word MAPS for map studies, MATH for excellent work and ZOO for animal reports.

A GREAT NATION - Display a large white scroll cut from butcher paper on the class bulletin board. Children can write papers explaining the need for good citizenship and love for our country.

Classroom Helpers

Give one boy or girl helper pattern to each child in class. The children can do their own coloring and cutting. Ask them to print their own name either on the bow or the baseball cap.

Label small envelopes with the names of classroom duties. Pin them to the class bulletin board. Slip the cute boy/girl helpers into the appropriate duty envelopes. Switch them weekly so each child can be included.

Mark

Jane

Flag salute

Line Leader

Turkey Pattern

NOVEMBER

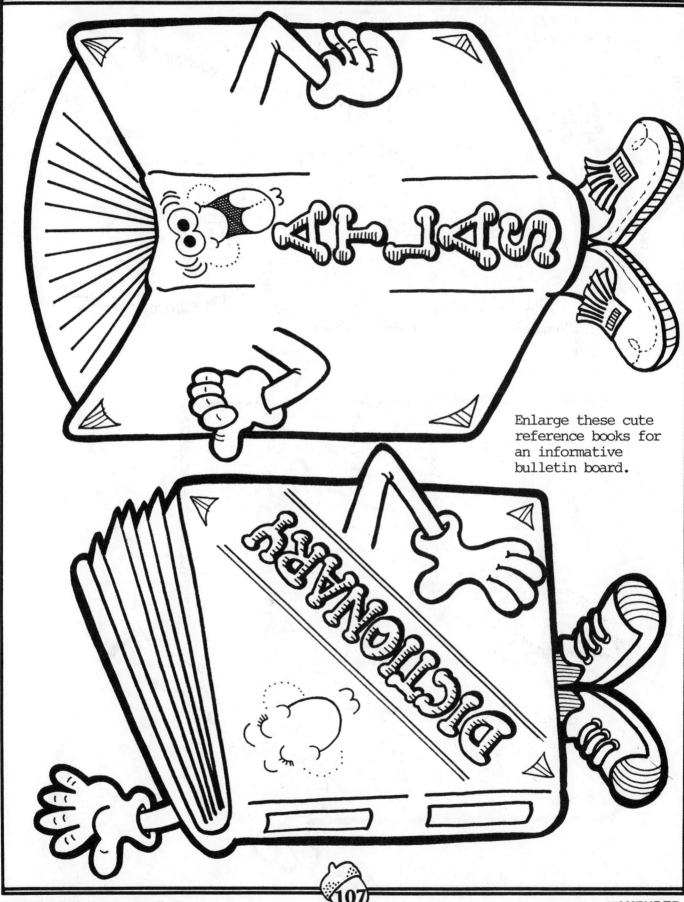

Enlarge these cute reference books for an informative bulletin board.

NOVEMBER

Notes

Answer Key

ACTIVITY 1

1. Washington
2. Oregon
3. California
4. Nevada
5. Idaho
6. Arizona
7. Utah
8. Montana
9. Wyoming
10. Colorado
11. New Mexico
12. North Dakota
13. South Dakota
14. Nebraska
15. Kansas
16. Oklahoma
17. Texas
18. Minnesota
19. Iowa
20. Missouri
21. Arkansas
22. Louisiana
23. Wisconsin
24. Illinois
25. Michigan
26. Indiana
27. Kentucky
28. Tennessee
29. Mississippi
30. Alabama
31. Ohio
32. West Virginia
33. Virginia
34. North Carolina
35. South Carolina
36. Georgia
37. Florida
38. Pennsylvania
39. New York
40. Vermont
41. New Hampshire
42. Maine
43. Massachusetts
44. Connecticut
45. Rhode Island
46. New Jersey
47. Delaware
48. Maryland
49. Alaska
50. Hawaii

ACTIVITY 2

FIND THESE ELECTION WORDS: NOVEMBER, PRESIDENT, VICE-PRESIDENT, VOTE, BALLOT, DEMOCRAT, REPUBLICAN, CANDIDATE, SPEECH, CAMPAIGN, CONVENTION, INAUGURATION, ELECTION, TERM, NATION.

```
S V R T G H Y K L H N S P E E C H F B N K L Y
X Z A S W Q R T H Y B H R D C V T Y H U J M H
D C X V C A N D I D A T E F H J I I L K M N G
V F G H O S X V B H L J S F T Y N A T I O N P
W R T Y N G H Y U I L N I B G H A R Y U I O P
C V G Y V H U I K J O R D S W E U C V C W Q E
Q S X D E G B F D R T U E D S W G F R A F V B
M L K O N O V E M B E R N O K J U J K M F G T
E L E C T I O N D R T Y T H N J R H G P C V B
R T Y U I S R T G H U J K I O L A G H A C X Z
L P O I O G F D E M O C R A T F T A W I D R T
S G H U N G H Y U I K M N H U Y I F T G E W Y
V I C E P R E S I D E N T F G T O F N N C E T
Q F R H G B N M K I L O H B G Y N R F D E W S
T E R M C D F R E P U B L I C A N F R H Y U K
E S C V T G B N J U I K M K L O P M N J H Y T
X D R T G V B H U J M N H Y T R E W Q A S D E
F R G B N J I U H J K L O P M N B V G F R Q W
```

STATES AND CAPITALS

Alabama	Montgomery	New York	Albany
Alaska	Juneau	North Carolina	Raleigh
Arizona	Phoenix	North Dakota	Bismark
Arkansas	Little Rock	Ohio	Columbus
California	Sacramento	Oklahoma	Oklahoma City
Colorado	Denver	Oregon	Salem
Connecticut	Hartford	Pennsylvania	Harrisburg
Delaware	Dover	Rhode Island	Providence
Florida	Tallahassee	South Carolina	Columbia
Georgia	Atlanta	South Dakota	Pierre
Hawaii	Honolulu	Tennessee	Nashville
Idaho	Boise	Texas	Austin
Illinois	Springfield	Utah	Salt Lake City
Indiana	Indianapolis	Vermont	Montpelier
Iowa	Des Moines	Virginia	Richmond
Kansas	Topeka	Washington	Olympia
Kentucky	Frankfort	West Virginia	Charleston
Louisiana	Baton Rouge	Wisconsin	Madison
Maine	Augusta	Wyoming	Cheyenne
Maryland	Annapolis		
Massachusetts	Boston		
Michigan	Lansing		
Minnesota	St. Paul		
Mississippi	Jackson		
Missouri	Jefferson City		
Montana	Helena		
Nebraska	Lincoln		
Nevada	Carson City		
New Hampshire	Concord		
New Jersey	Trenton		
New Mexico	Santa Fe		

NOVEMBER